Dwarf Panda

"Teaching a child not to step on a caterpillar is as valuable to the child as it is to the caterpillar."

BRADLEY MILLER

DEDICATION

To Bowie my love,
thank you for sticking around for 15 years
so I could be your mom.

Chimpanzee

Chimpanzees are highly intelligent primates known for their social nature and remarkable problem-solving abilities.

Mountain Gorilla

Mountain gorillas are the largest primates on earth, with males weighing up to 440 pounds, and they have been observed using tools such as sticks and leaves to gather food and water.

Giant Panda

Their pseudo-thumb is actually an enlarged wrist bone that helps them grip bamboo with incredible dexterity.

Saiga Antelope

Their flexible snout helps them filter out dust and warm up cold winter air before it reaches their lungs.

Red Panda

Not a bear, but rather a unique and solitary species that is closely related to raccoons, weasels, and skunks.

African Elephant

The largest land animals in the world, they are known for their amazing memories and complex social structures.

Philippine Eagle

Their sharp talons can exert a force
five times stronger than that of a
human hand.

Saiga Antelope

Known for their distinctive appearance, with an elongated snout and large, downturned horns.

Green Turtle

Can grow up to 5 feet long and weigh over 300 pounds.

Giant Chinese Salamander

Completely aquatic with lungs and the ability to absorb oxygen through their skin, making them excellent divers.

Philippine Eagle

With a wingspan of up to seven feet, they have the ability to hunt prey as large as monkeys and flying lemurs.

Giant Hairy-Nosed Wombat

A unique and mysterious marsupial, with a face that looks like a cross between a bear and a pig.

African Wild Dog

They have a unique coat pattern that is different for every individual, making it easier to identify them.

Vaquita "Panda of the Sea"

The smallest and rarest porpoise in the world, with less than 30 individuals remaining in the wild.

Amur Leopard

A skilled climber, they are able to
drag prey much larger than
themselves up trees to protect it
from other predators.

African Wild Dog

These social animals are also skilled hunters, and they use coordinated tactics to chase and capture their prey.

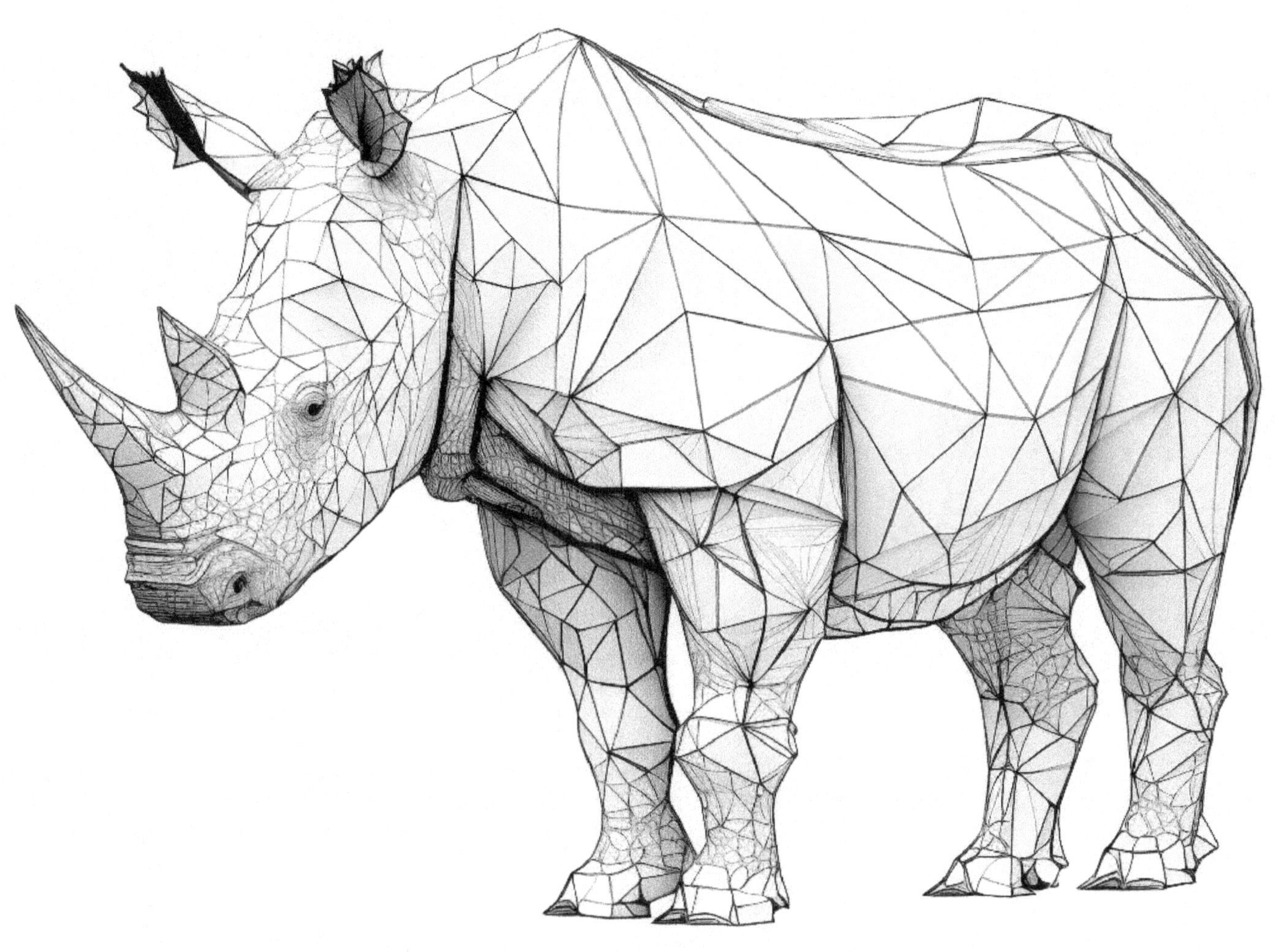

Black Rhinoceros

They have poor eyesight but a great sense of smell and hearing, which helps them detect predators and locate food in their environment.

Vaquita Dolphin

Known for their distinctive facial expressions and permanent smile, they are one of the cutest marine animals in the world.

Giant Panda

Despite their heavy weight, pandas can easily climb trees and are actually quite skilled at it.

Pangolin

The pangolin's unique scales are made of keratin, the same material as human hair and nails.

The White Rhino

The white rhino is not actually white - it's gray!

Giant Hairy-Nosed Wombat

A nocturnal animal that feeds on grass, bark, and roots, and can dig burrows up to 100 feet long.

Hawksbill Turtle

Has a unique shell structure that allows it to access and feed on sponges, which makes up a significant portion of their diet.

Panda Mama and Cubs

Mother pandas have a special bond with their cubs and will often cradle them in their arms for hours on end, grooming and cuddling them with love and care.

THANKS *for reading*